MW01244728

This books belongs to

- .

Thank you for buying this book.

We have taken great care in its production.

We hope this book will provide your child with some enjoyable coloring sessions.

Feel free to leave us a comment on the Amazon product page.

Your opinion is important. It will allow others to discover this book.

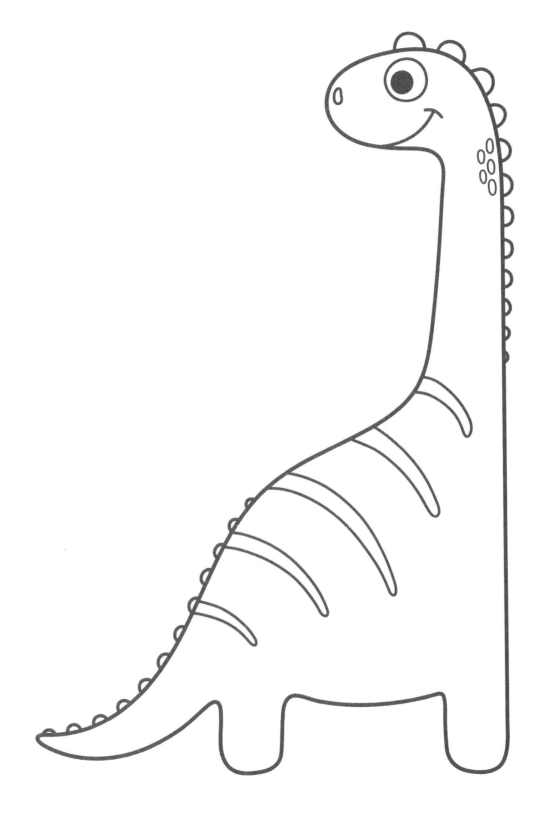

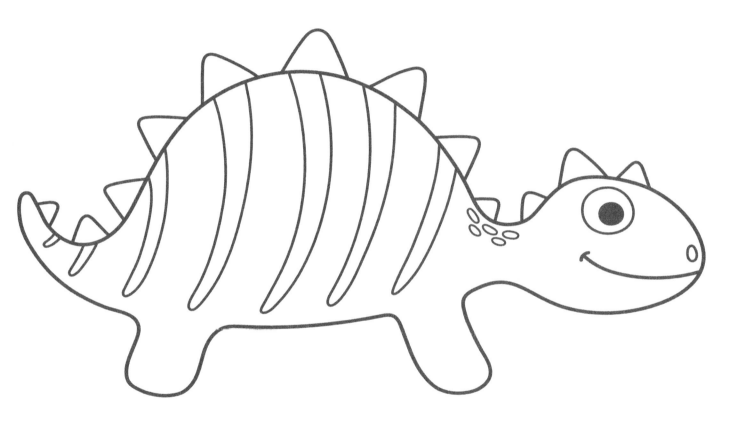

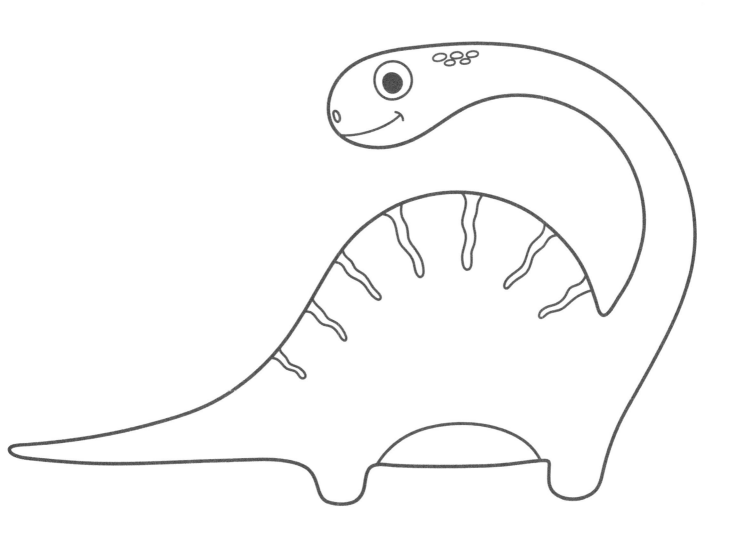

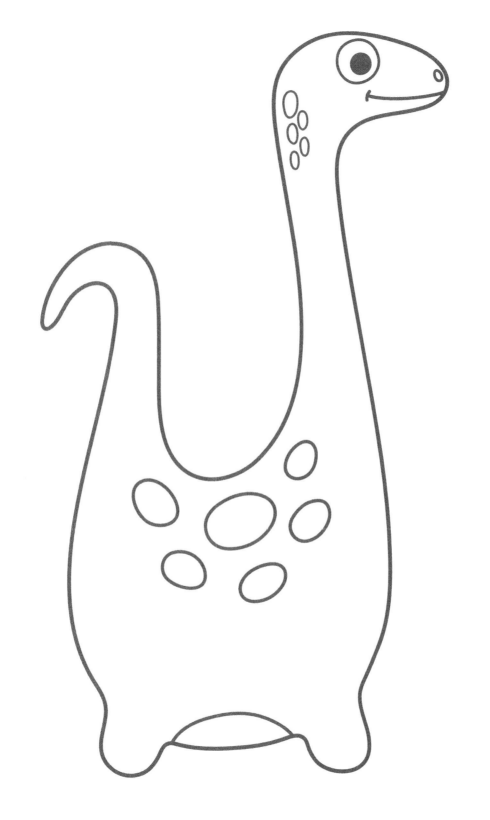

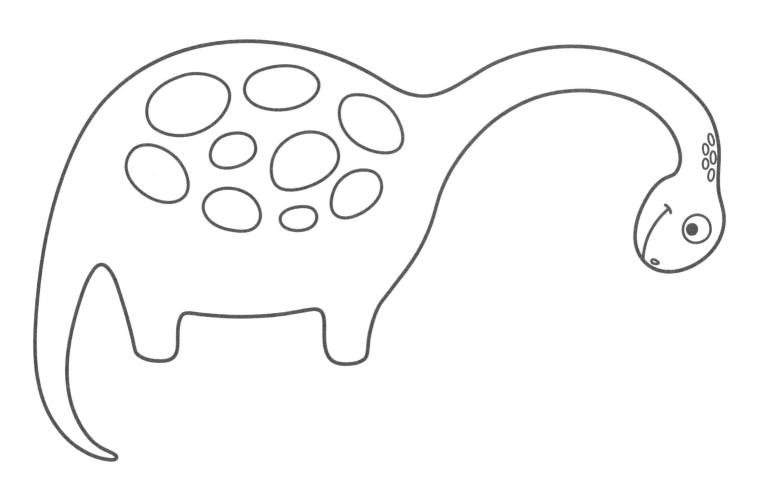

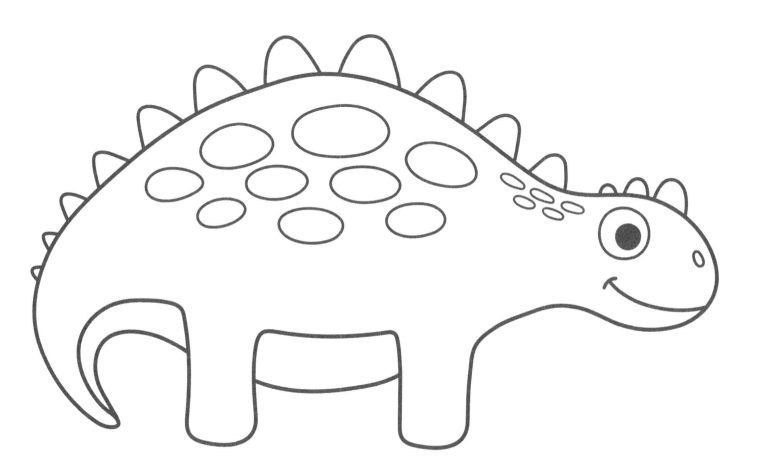

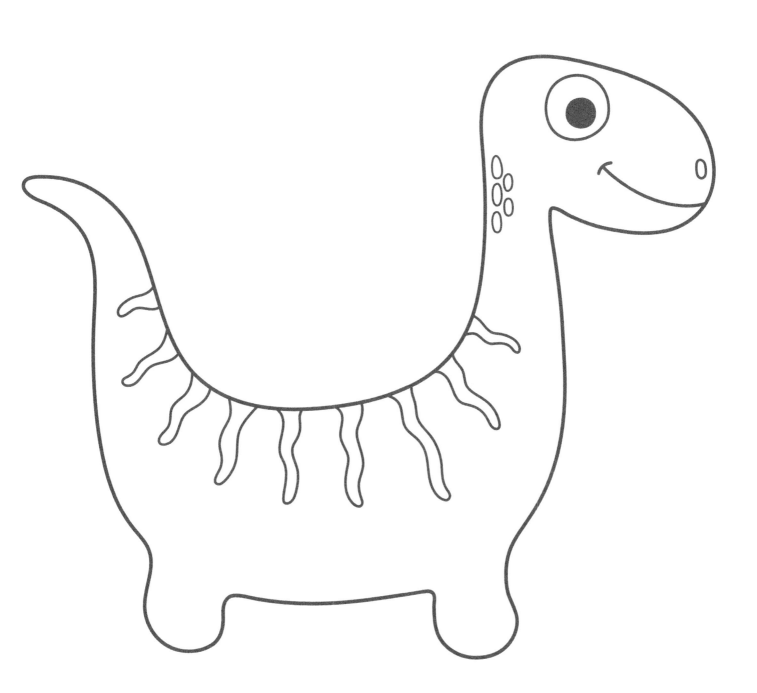

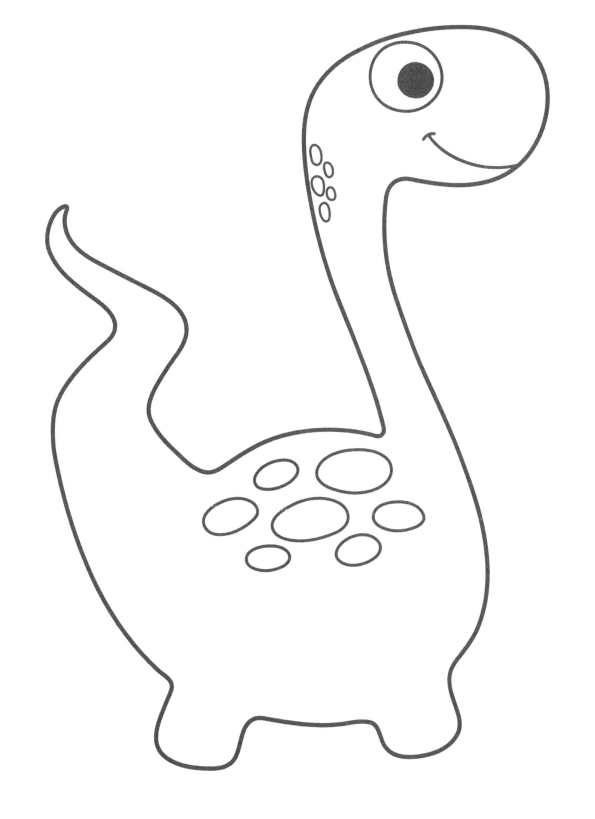

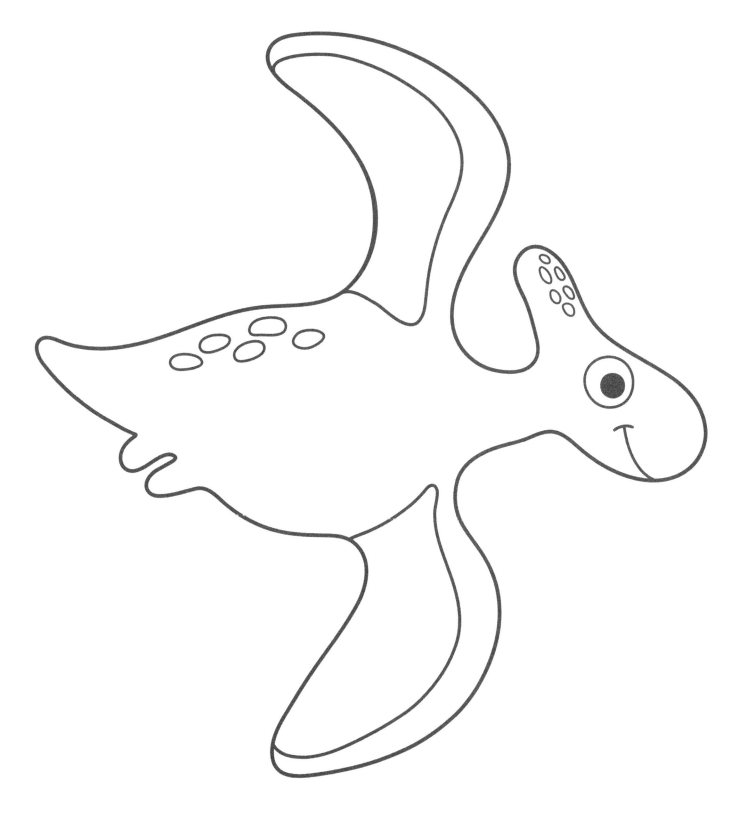

Made in the USA
Middletown, DE
16 October 2023

40949786R00057